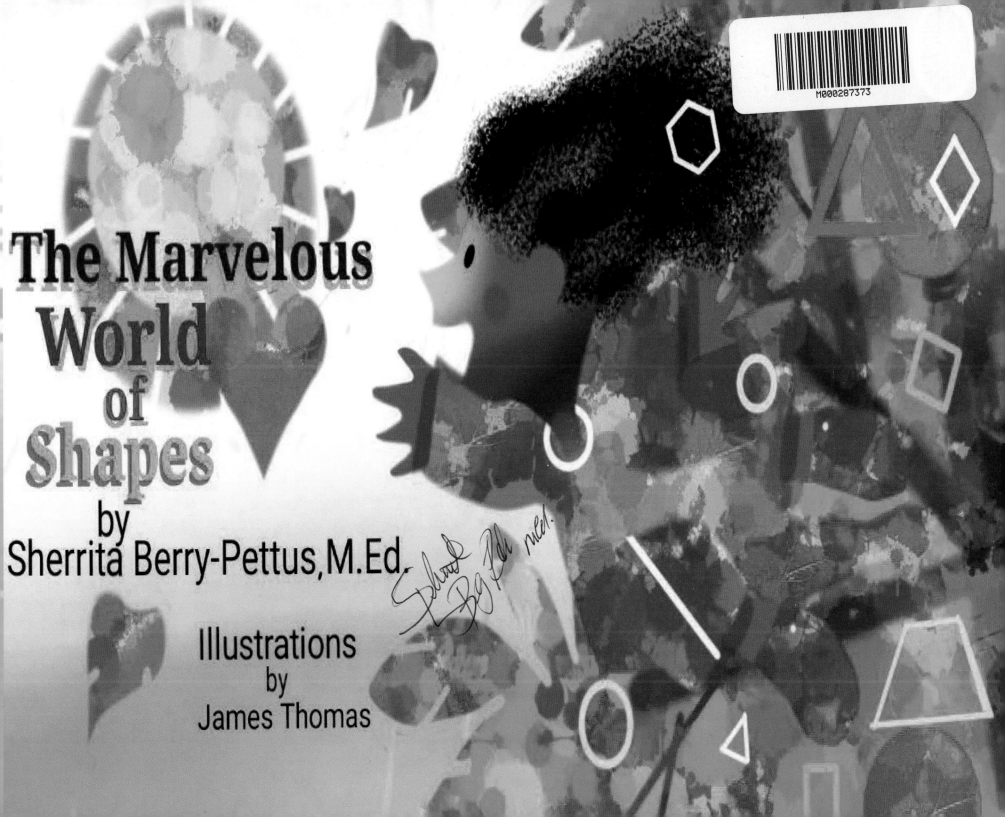

The Marvelous World of Shapes

by

Sherrita Berry-Pettus, M.Ed.

Illustrations
by
James Thomas

www.booksbymrsberry-pettus.com

First Edition: January 13, 2019
Printed in the United States of America
ISBN: 978-1-945342-12-7

Shapes, shapes, shapes!
I love finding shapes!

What shape do you see?
Triangle!

Shapes, shapes, shapes!
I love finding shapes!

What shape do you see?
Square!

Shapes, shapes, shapes!
I love finding shapes!

What shape do you see?
Circle!

Shapes, shapes, shapes!
I love finding shapes!

What shape do you see?
Rectangle!

Shapes, shapes, shapes!
I love finding shapes!

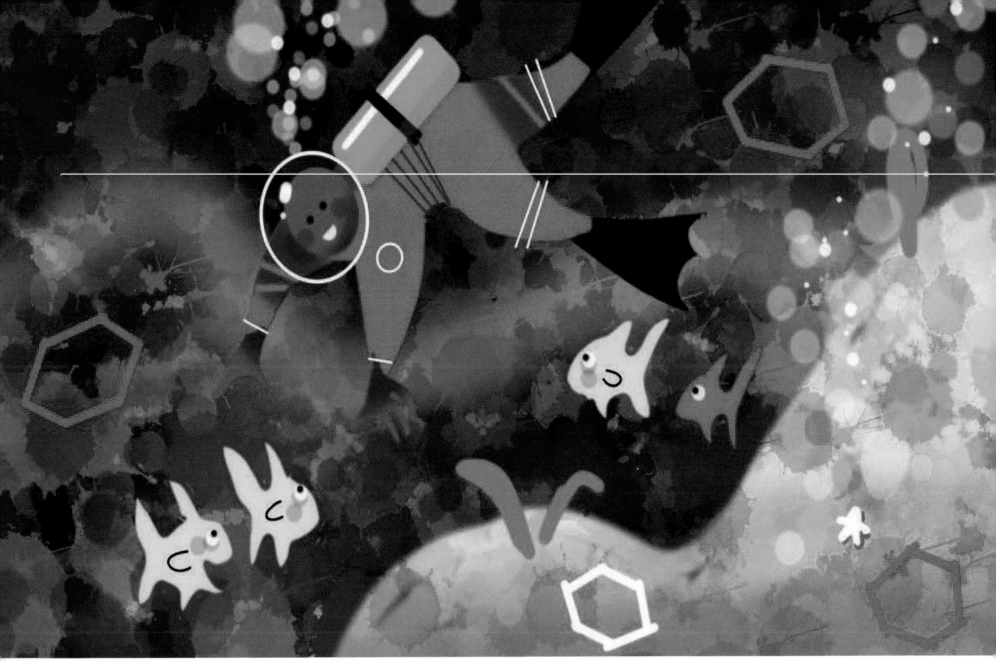

What shape do you see?
Hexagon!

Shapes, shapes, shapes!
I love finding shapes!

What shape do you see?
Rhombus

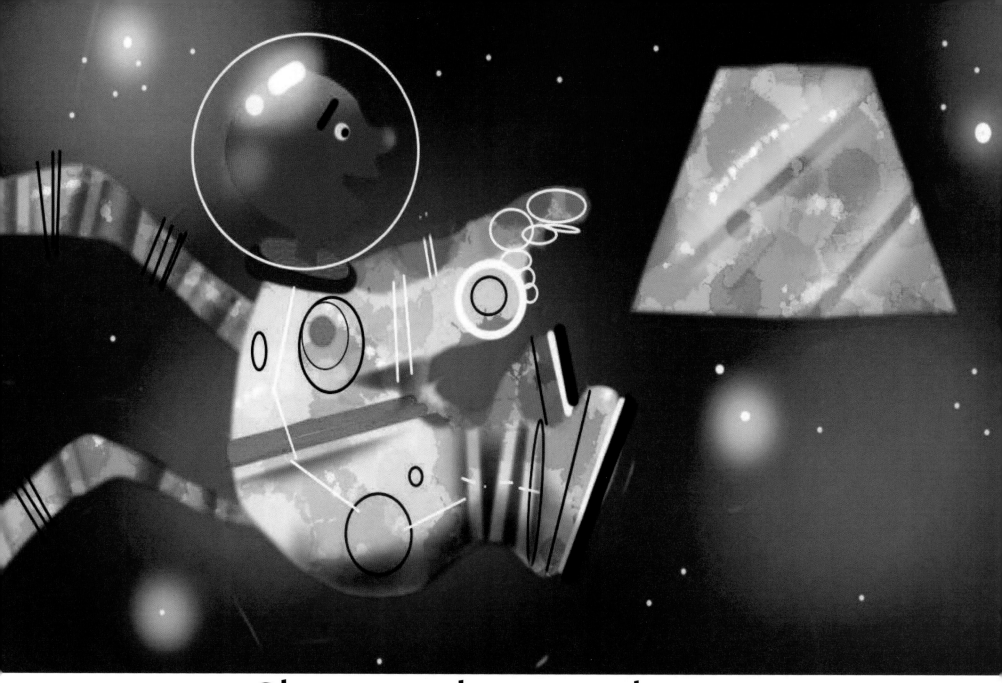

Shapes, shapes, shapes!
I love finding shapes!

What shape do you see?
Trapezoid!

Shapes, shapes, shapes! I love finding shapes!
How many shapes do you see in this picture?

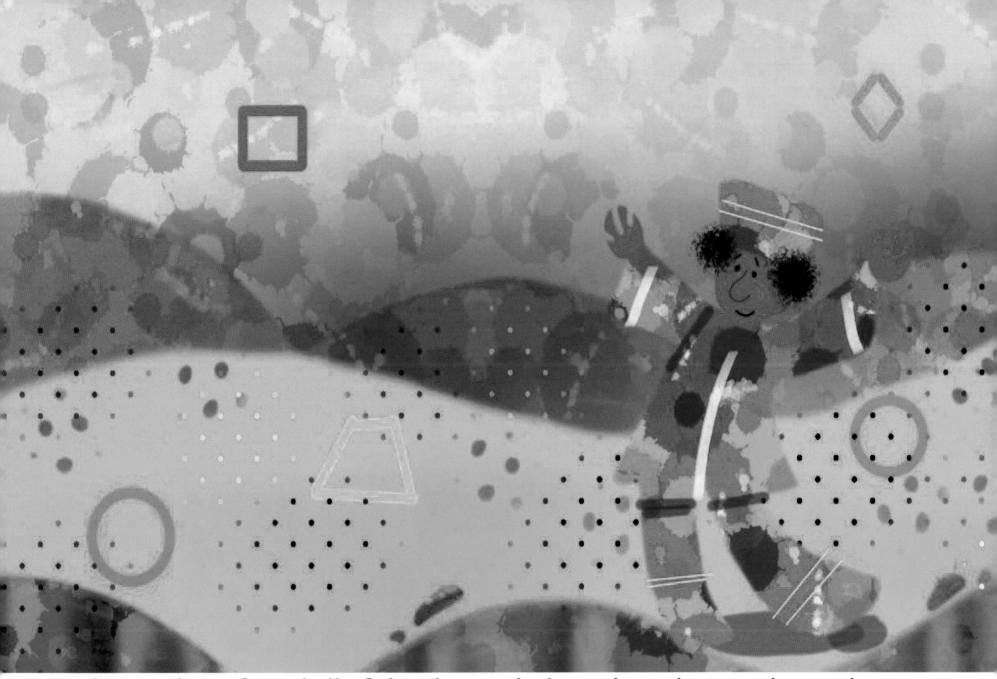

Now that we have found all of the shapes, let's explore them and see what we can learn about them! When you look at each shape, count how many sides and corners they have. **Are you ready? Let's go!**

Shapes, shapes, shapes! Let's explore the **triangle**!
Did you count **three** sides and **three** corners?
Terrific job! Let's move on to the next shape!

Shapes, shapes, shapes! Let's explore the **square**!
Did you count **four equal** sides and **four** corners? Fantastic job! Let's move on to the next shape!

Shapes, shapes, shapes! Let's explore the **circle**! Did you find any sides? Of course not, silly! Circles have **zero** sides and **zero** corners. Great job! Let's move on to the next shape!

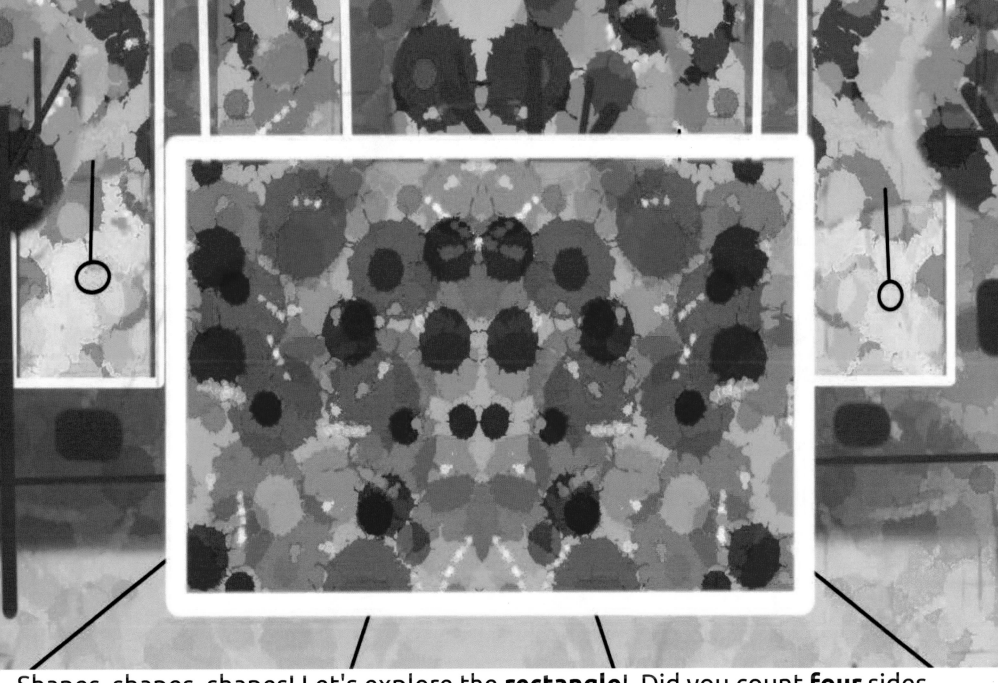

Shapes, shapes, shapes! Let's explore the **rectangle**! Did you count **four** sides and **four** corners? Exceptional job! Rectangles are special because they have **two matching pairs**. Let's move on to the next shape!

Shapes, shapes, shapes! Let's explore the **hexagon**!
Did you count **six** sides and **six** corners? Amazing job!
Let's move on to the next shape!

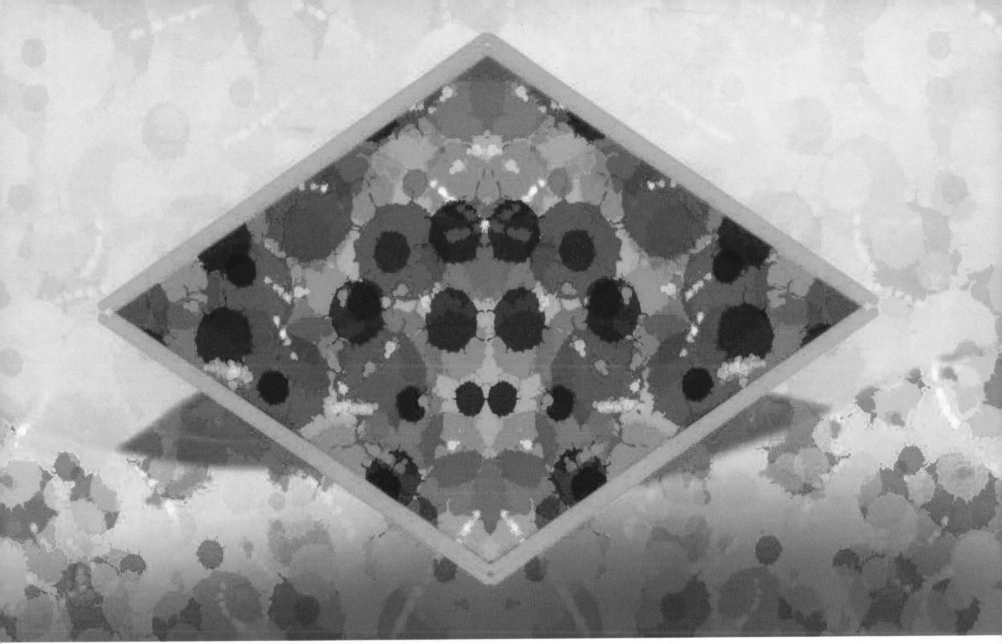

Shapes, shapes, shapes! Let's explore the **rhombus**!

Did you count **four equal** sides and **four** corners? Terrific job!

Did you know that another name for a rhombus is a diamond?

Cool! Let's move on to the next shape!

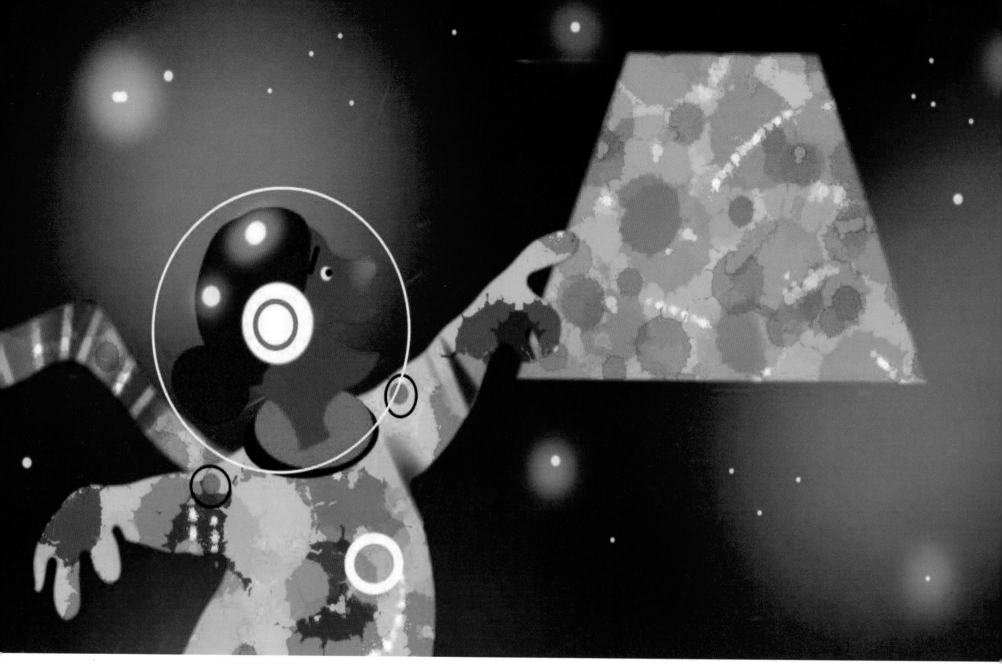

Shapes, shapes, shapes!

Let's explore the **trapezoid**!

Did you count **four** sides and **four** corners?

Tremendous job! Trapezoids are unique in the shape world because they have a set of parallel sides. This means the sides will never run into each other.

The shapes we discovered today are called **2D** shapes in the math world. **All 2D shapes are flat**. Please remember this fact.

All 2D shapes are what?
Flat.... and that's a fact!

Now that you know all of the primary shapes, you are ready to find shapes in the marvelous world we live in!

Bye, bye!

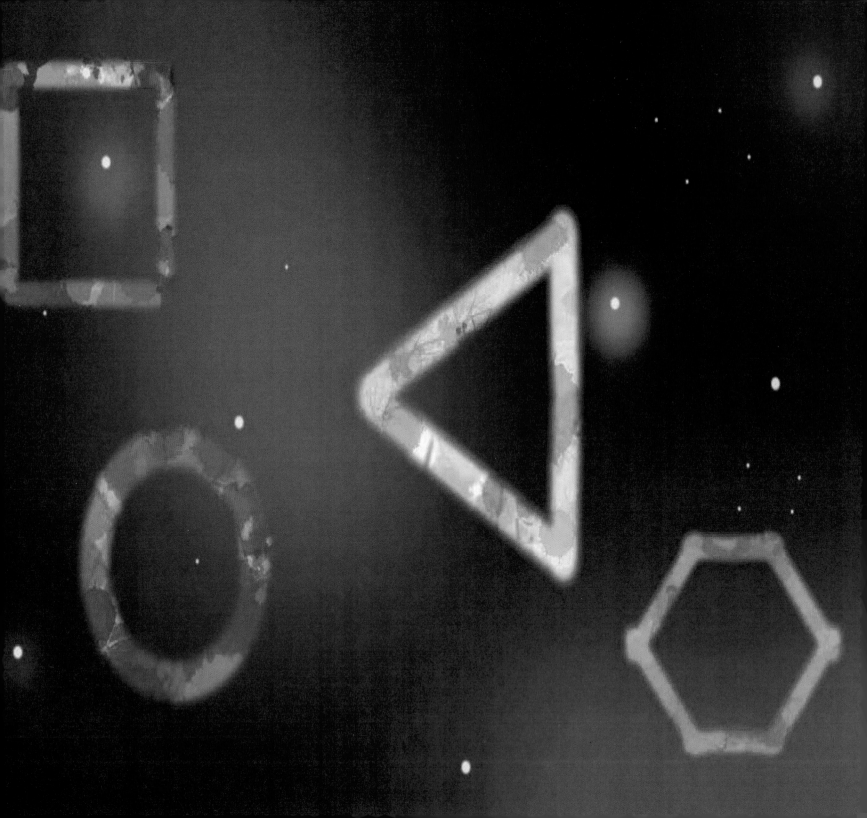

Note to parents and teachers:
Here are a few ideas and recommendations on how to use this book with young learners.

- For introducing the shapes, read up to page 16.
- To learn more about the shapes, including their attributes, read the entire book.
- To further extend your child's learning, go on a scavenger hunt outside, around your house, around the classroom or school.

Teachers: This book can be used to supplement a two or three day lesson.

Day One- Introduce the shapes by reading up to page 16.

Day Two- Read the second half of the book, starting at page 17, to learn and explore the attributes of the 2D shapes in the book.

Day Three- Review the shapes and their attributes by reading the whole book and having the students answer questions.